WARNING

When I am an old woman
I shall wear purple

JENNY JOSEPH

•

Illustrated by Pythia Ashton-Jewell

SOUVENIR PRESS

When I am an old woman

I shall wear purple
With a red hat which doesn't go, and
doesn't suit me.

And I shall spend my pension on
                brandy and summer gloves
And satin sandals, and say we've
                   no money for butter.

I shall sit down on the pavement
when I'm tired

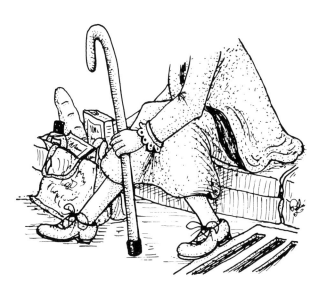

And gobble up samples in shops

and press alarm bells

And run my stick along the public
railings

And make up for the sobriety
of my youth.

I shall go out in my slippers in the

                                                  rain

And pick the flowers in other
                                    people's gardens
And learn to spit.

You can wear terrible shirts **and**
grow more fat
And eat three pounds of sausages
at a go
Or only bread and pickle for a week

And hoard pens and pencils and
beermats and things in boxes.

But now we must have clothes that
                    keep us dry
And pay our rent and not swear in
                    the street

And set a good example for the
children.

We must have friends to dinner and
read the papers.

But maybe I ought to practise
a little now?

So people who know me are not too
shocked and surprised
When suddenly I am old, and start
to wear purple.

WARNING

When I am an old woman I shall
                     wear purple
With a red hat which doesn't go, and
                     doesn't suit me.
And I shall spend my pension on
                brandy and summer gloves
And satin sandals, and say we've no
                  money for butter.
I shall sit down on the pavement
                  when I'm tired
And gobble up samples in shops and
                  press alarm bells
And run my stick along the public
                    railings
And make up for the sobriety of my
                    youth.
I shall go out in my slippers in the
                    rain
And pick the flowers in other
                people's gardens
And learn to spit.

You can wear terrible shirts and grow
                                 more fat
And eat three pounds of sausages at
                                    a go
Or only bread and pickle for a week
And hoard pens and pencils and
                beermats and things in boxes.

But now we must have clothes **that**
                            keep us dry
And pay our rent and not swear in
                              the street
And set a good example for the
                               children.
We must have friends to dinner and
                       read the papers.

But maybe I ought to practise a little
                                  now?
So people who know me are not too
                 shocked and surprised
When suddenly I am old, and start to
                        wear purple.

This edition first published 1997 by
Souvenir Press Ltd.,
43 Great Russell Street, London WC1B 3PD

Reprinted 1998, 1999, (twice), 2000(twice),
2001(4times), 2002(5times), 2003(6times),
2004(8times), 2005(3times), 2006(3times),
2007, 2008, 2009 (twice), Reprinted 2010,2011,2013

ISBN (13) 9780285634114

Typeset in Meridien by
Rowland Phototypesetting Ltd.,
Bury St Edmunds, Suffolk
Printed in Malaysia